Phonics Readiness

Preschool

Published by Spectrum
an imprint of Carson-Dellosa Publishing LLC
Greensboro, NC

Spectrum is an imprint of Carson-Dellosa Publishing.

Printed in the United States of America. All rights reserved. Except as permitted under the United States Copyright Act, no part of this publication may be reproduced or distributed in any form or by any means, or stored in a database or retrieval system, without prior written permission from the publisher, unless otherwise indicated. Spectrum is an imprint of Carson-Dellosa Publishing. © 2011 Carson-Dellosa Publishing.

Send all inquiries to:
Carson-Dellosa Publishing
P.O. Box 35665
Greensboro, NC 27425

Printed in Versailles, KY USA   ISBN 978-1-60996-204-3

03-237147811

Table of Contents

Letter **Aa** 5
Letter **Bb** 6
Letter **Cc** 7
Letter **Dd** 8
Review Five Little Monkeys 9
Letter **Ee** 11
Letter **Ff** 12
Letter **Gg** 13
Letter **Hh** 14
Review Good Night 15
Letter **Ii** 17
Letter **Jj** 18
Letter **Kk** 19
Letter **Ll** 20
Review Mary Had a Little Lamb 21
Letter **Mm** 23
Letter **Nn** 24
Letter **Oo** 25
Letter **Pp** 26
Review Pat a Cake 27
Letter **Qq** 29
Letter **Rr** 30
Letter **Ss** 31
Letter **Tt** 32
Letter **Uu** 33
Review Six Little Ducks 34
Letter **Vv** 36
Letter **W** 37
Letter **Xx** 38
Letter **Yy** 39
Letter **Zz** 40
Review Alphabet Song 41
Post Test 43
Beginning Sound of **Bb** 45
Ending Sound of **Bb** 46
Beginning Sound of **Cc** 47
Ending Sound of **Cc** 48
Beginning Sound of **Dd** 49
Ending Sound of **Dd** 50
Review Beginning Sounds of **Bb, Cc, Dd** 51
Review Ending Sounds of **Bb, Cc, Dd** 52
Beginning Sound of **Ff** 53
Ending Sound of **Ff** 54
Beginning Sound of **Gg** 55
Ending Sound of **Gg** 56
Beginning Sound of **Hh** 57

Review Beginning Sounds of **Ff**, **Gg**, **Hh** 58
Review Ending Sounds of **Ff**, **Gg** 59
Beginning Sound of **Jj** 60
Ending Sound of **Jj** 61
Beginning Sound of **Kk** 62
Ending Sound of **Kk** 63
Beginning Sound of **Ll** 64
Ending Sound of **Ll** 65
Review Beginning Sounds of **Jj**, **Kk**, **Ll** 66
Review Ending Sounds of **Jj**, **Kk**, **Ll** 67
Beginning Sound of **Mm** 68
Ending Sound of **Mm** 69
Beginning Sound of **Nn** 70
Ending Sound of **Nn** 71
Beginning Sound of **Pp** 72
Ending Sound of **Pp** 73
Review Beginning Sounds of **Mm**, **Nn**, **Pp** 74
Review Ending Sounds of **Mm**, **Nn**, **Pp** 75
Beginning Sound of **Qq** 76
Beginning Sound of **Rr** 77
Ending Sound of **Rr** 78
Beginning Sound of **Ss** 79
Ending Sound of **Ss** 80
Review Beginning Sounds of **Qq**, **Rr**, **Ss** 81
Review Ending Sounds of **Rr** and **Ss** 82
Beginning Sound of **Tt** 83
Ending Sound of **Tt** 84
Beginning Sound of **Vv** 85
Beginning Sound of **Ww** 86
Review Beginning Sounds of **Tt**, **Vv**, **Ww** 87
Review Ending Sounds of **Tt** 88
Beginning Sound of **Xx** 89
Ending Sound of **Xx** 90
Beginning Sound of **Yy** 91
Beginning Sound of **Zz** 92
Ending Sound of **Zz** 93
Review Beginning Sounds of **Xx**, **Yy**, **Zz** 94
Review Ending Sounds of **Xx** and **Zz** 95
Post Test Beginning Sounds 96
Post Test Ending Sounds 97
Long **a** Sound 98
Long **e** Sound 99
Long **i** Sound 100
Long **o** Sound 101
Long **u** Sound 102
Review Long **a**, **e**, **i** Sounds 103
Review Long **o** and **u** Sounds 104
Answer Key 105

Letter Aa

Directions: Name the pictures out loud. Then, circle the **a** in each name.

apple   grapes   ant

yarn   hat   pan

ball   alligator   ax

Letter Bb

Directions: Name the pictures out loud. Then, circle the **b** in each name.

book

rabbit

zebra

bee

comb

bird

Name _____

Letter Cc

Directions: Name the pictures out loud. Then, color the **c** in each name.

| c | a | r | r | o | t |

| d | u | c | k |

| c | o | m | b |

| o | c | t | o | p | u | s |

| w | a | t | c | h |

| s | c | i | s | s | o | r | s |

Letter Dd

Directions: Name the pictures out loud. Then, circle the **d** in each name.

deer

bird

sled

bed

duck

lid

dime

bread

Review: Five Little Monkeys

Directions: Read "Five Little Monkeys" to your child. Hold up five fingers and bounce them up and down to act out "jumping on the bed." When you say "bumped his head" hold your head. Next ask your child to say and act out the finger play with you.

Five little monkeys jumping on the bed,

One fell off and bumped his head.

Four little monkeys jumping on the bed,

One fell off and bumped his head.

Three little monkeys jumping on the bed,

One fell off and bumped his head.

Two little monkeys jumping on the bed,

One fell off and bumped his head.

One little monkey jumping on the bed,

He fell off and bumped his head.

Review: Five Little Monkeys

Directions: Underline each **a**, **b**, and **d** that you find below.

Five little monkeys jumping on the bed,

One fell off and bumped his head.

Four little monkeys jumping on the bed,

One fell off and bumped his head.

Three little monkeys jumping on the bed,

One fell off and bumped his head.

Two little monkeys jumping on the bed,

One fell off and bumped his head.

One little monkey jumping on the bed,

He fell off and bumped his head.

Letter Ee

Directions: Name all the body parts. Then, circle the **e** in each name. Next, draw a line from each body part to where it would be on the boy.

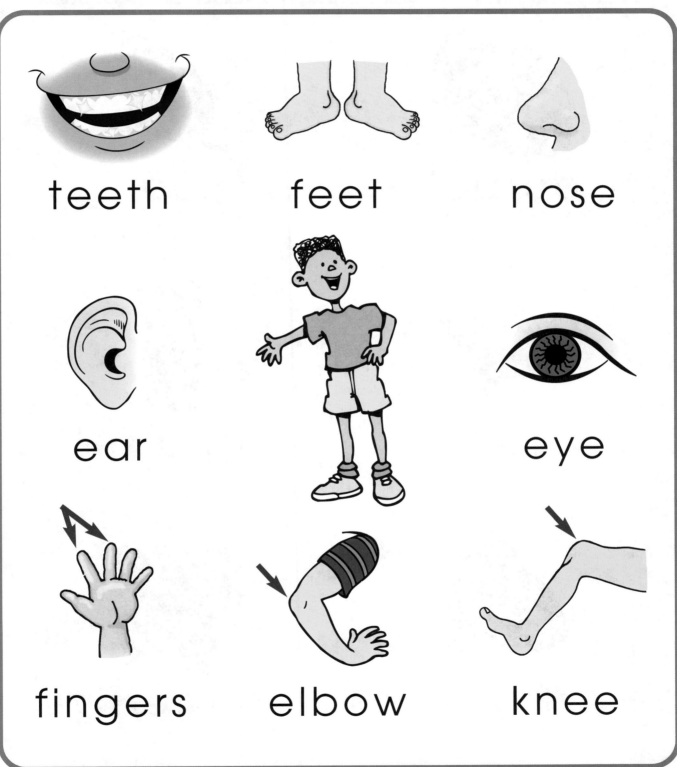

teeth   feet   nose

ear   eye

fingers   elbow   knee

Letter Ff

Directions: Name all the pictures. Then, circle the **f** in each name.

football

leaf

fox

giraffe

frog

butterfly

Letter Gg

Directions: Name all the pictures. Then, circle the **g** in each name.

grapes

yogurt

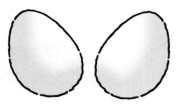

eggs

orange

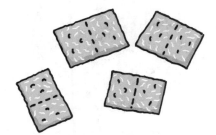

graham crackers

Letter Hh

Directions: Name all the pictures. Then, circle the **h** in each picture name.

horn

horse

house

fish

sandwich

hat

elephant

Review

Directions: Read the poem "Good Night" out loud. Then, find and underline the words that rhyme.

Good night, sleep tight.

Wake up bright

In the morning light

To do what's right

With all your might.

Name _____

Review

Directions: Name the letter at the beginning of each row. Then, name all the pictures in the row. Circle the letter in each word that matches the letter at the beginning of the row.

Ee	egg	elephant	leg
Ff	giraffe	leaf	calf
Gg	flag	bag	goose
Hh	horn	fish	dish

Letter Ii

Directions: Say the name of each picture. Then, circle the **i** in each name.

bike   milk

fish   bird

ice cream   ice cube

Letter Jj

Directions: Say the name of each picture. Then, underline each **j** you find.

banjo   pajamas   jam

jet

jump rope

monkey

juice

Name _____

Letter Kk

Directions: Say the name of each picture. Then, circle the **k** in each name. Underline each animal.

key

duck   fork   kitten

bike

Letter Ll

Directions: Say the name of each picture. Then, underline the l in each name.

lock

butterfly

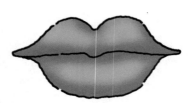

lips

balloon

pencil

lamb

candle

apple

lamp

Review

Directions: Read "Mary Had a Little Lamb." Then, underline the rhyming words in the poem.

Mary Had a Little Lamb

Mary had a little lamb

With fleece as white as snow.

And everywhere that Mary went,

The lamb was sure to go!

It followed her to school one day,

which was against the rule.

It made the children laugh and play,

To see a lamb at school.

Review

Directions: Say the name of the letter at the beginning of each row. Then, circle the letter in each picture name. Color each picture that could be in Mary's school.

Ii	bike	pig	milk
Jj	jacket	jet	pajamas
Kk	kite	king	blanket
Ll	flag	lamb	pencil

Name _____

Letter Mm

Directions: Say the name of each picture. Then, draw a line under the **m** in each name. Draw an **X** on each animal.

milk

lamb

drum

nut

moon

moose

mouse

dime

monkey

Letter Nn

Directions: Say the name of each picture. Then, draw a line under the **n** in each name.

hen

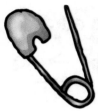
pin

pan

bun

man

fan

nut

van

can

Letter Oo

Directions: Say the name of each picture. Then, circle the **o** in each name.

rose

fox

doll

orange

bone

nose

top

sock

Letter Pp

Directions: Say the name of each picture. Then, circle the **p** in each name. Underline each piece of fruit.

pony   grapes   apple

tape   pen   pig

peach   pineapple   pear

Review

Directions: Read "Pat-a-Cake." Underline the words that rhyme.

Pat-a-Cake

Pat-a-cake, pat-a-cake, baker's man,

Bake me a cake as fast as you can.

Pat it and smooth it and mark it with a **B**,

And put it in the oven for baby and me.

Review

Directions: Circle each **m**, **n**, **o**, and **p** in the poem.

Pat-a-Cake

Pat-a-cake, pat-a-cake, baker's man,

Bake me a cake as fast as you can.

Pat it and smooth it and mark it with a **B**,

And put it in the oven for baby and me.

Name _____

Letter Qq

Directions: Say the name of each picture. Then, circle the **q** in each name.

quarter quilt queen

quack question quail

squid quiet square

Name_____

Letter Rr

Directions: Say the name of each picture. Then, color the **r** in each name. Circle each thing that rolls.

r | a | c | c | o | o | n

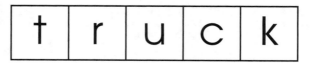

t | r | u | c | k

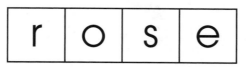

r | o | s | e

t | r | a | i | n

c | a | r

Letter Ss

Directions: Say the name of each picture. Then, circle the **s** in each name.

snake

spider

snail

starfish

fish

moose

horse

skunk

seal

Letter Tt

Directions: Say the name of each picture. Then, draw a line under the **t** in each name.

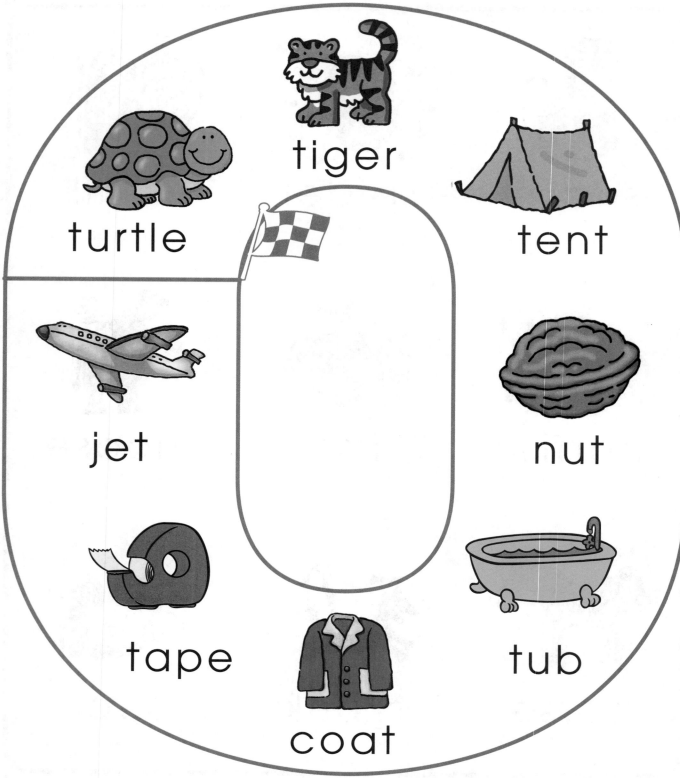

turtle

tiger

tent

jet

nut

tape

coat

tub

Letter Uu

Directions: Say the name of each picture. Then, circle the **u** in each name.

 umbrella

 bus

 rug

 tub

 drum

 sun

 puppy

 unhappy

 brush

Review

Directions: Read "Six Little Ducks." Then, underline the words that rhyme.

Six Little Ducks

Six little ducks that I once knew;

Black ones, brown ones, white ones, too.

But the one little duck with the feather on his back,

He led the others with a *quack, quack, quack.*

quack, quack, quack—quack, quack, quack.

He led the others with a *quack, quack, quack.*

Review

Directions: Circle each **q**, **r**, **s**, **t**, and **u** in the poem.

Six Little Ducks

Six little ducks that I once knew;

Black ones, brown ones, white ones, too.

But the one little duck with the feather on his back,

He led the others with a *quack, quack, quack.*

quack, quack, quack—quack, quack, quack.

He led the others with a *quack, quack, quack.*

Letter Vv

Directions: Name all the pictures. Then, circle the **v** in each name.

cave

van

vest

dive

vine

wave

vase

hive

violin

Letter Ww

Directions: Name all the pictures. Then, circle the **w** in each name.

wave

swim

snow

sweater

crown

whistle

watch

swing

wash

Name _____

Letter Xx

Directions: Name all the pictures. Then, color the **x** in each name.

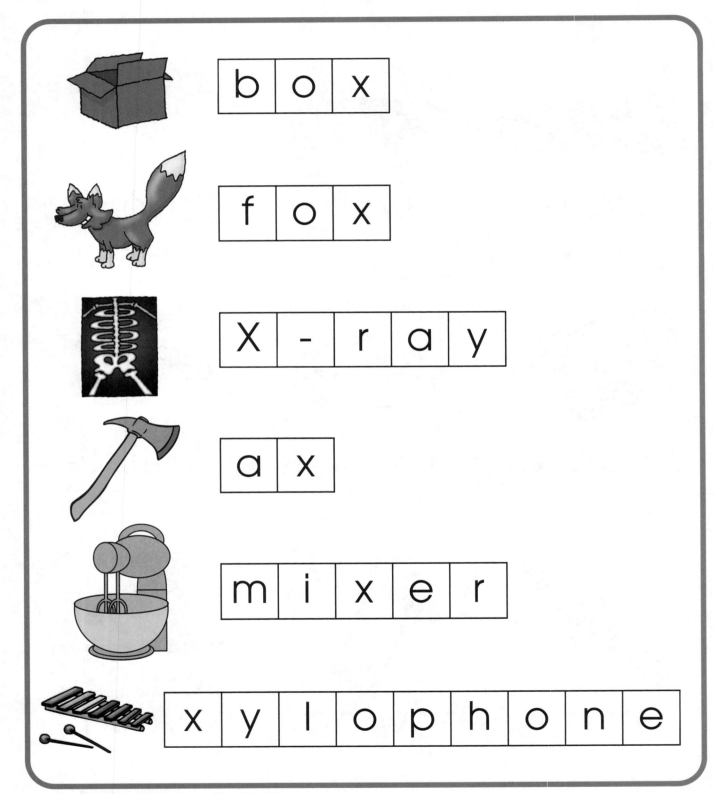

b	o	x

f	o	x

X	-	r	a	y

a	x

m	i	x	e	r

x	y	l	o	p	h	o	n	e

Letter Yy

Directions: Name all the pictures. Then, circle the **y** in each name.

pony

puppy

lady

yawn

sky

cry

yo-yo

yarn

baby

Name _____

Letter Zz

Directions: Name all the pictures. Then, color the **z** in each name.

z	i	p	p	e	r

z	e	b	r	a

l	i	z	a	r	d

m	a	g	a	z	i	n	e

Alphabet Song Review

Directions: Sing the "Alphabet Song."

A, B, C, D, E, F, G,

H, I, J, K, L, M, N, O, P,

Q, R, S,

T, U, V,

W, X, Y, **and** Z.

Now, I know my ABC's.

Next time won't you sing with me?

Alphabet Review

Directions: Draw a line to match the uppercase and lowercase letters.

A •		•	p
B •		•	m
C •		•	q
D •		•	o
E •		•	z
F •		•	l
G •		•	k
H •		•	v
I •		•	s
J •		•	r
K •		•	u
L •		•	t
M •		•	x
N •		•	c
O •		•	y
P •		•	w
Q •		•	n
R •		•	e
S •		•	i
T •		•	f
U •		•	g
V •		•	h
W •		•	a
X •		•	b
Y •		•	d
Z •		•	j

Chapter 1 Post-Test

Directions: Name all the letters and pictures. Then, find the letter in each name and draw a line under it.

Aa apple

Bb bee

Cc sock

Dd sled

Ee egg

Ff fish

Gg flag

Hh hat

Ii milk

Jj jam

Kk kangaroo

Ll plate

Mm monkey

Chapter I Post-Test

Directions: Name all the letters and pictures. Then, find the letter in each name and draw a line under it.

Nn pan	Uu bus
Oo doll	Vv vase
Pp tape	Ww snow
Qq queen	Xx box
Rr frog	Yy puppy
Ss saw	Zz zebra
Tt tiger	

Beginning Sound of Bb

Directions: Listen to the /b/ sound at the beginning of **boy**, **bat**, and **ball**. Circle the names that begin with the /b/ sound.

This **b**oy can **b**at the **b**all.

balloon   cat   banana

bat   car   ball

dog   bed   bell

Name _____

Ending Sound of Bb

Directions: Read the sentence and listen to the /b/ sound at the end of **scrub** and **tub**. Then, circle the pictures that end with the /b/ sound.

 I will scru**b** the tu**b**.

tub

crab

mug

bib

web

tape

taxicab

red

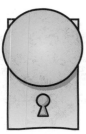

doorknob

Beginning Sounds of Cc

Directions: When **c** comes at the beginning of a word, sometimes it makes an /s/ sound and sometimes it makes a /k/ sound. Say each word out loud. Underline the pictures that begin with a **c** that makes an /s/ sound. Then, circle the pictures that begin with a **c** that makes the /k/ sound.

city   can   car

dog   circle   bird

cent   doll   cat

Ending Sound of Cc

Directions: When **c** is at the end of a word, it makes the /k/ sound. Say each word out loud. Circle each picture that ends with a **c** that makes the /k/ sound.

traffic

garlic

picnic

tub

bed

pig

Beginning Sound of Dd

Directions: Read the words out loud. Cross out any picture that does not begin with the /d/ sound.

dime   duck

brush   drum   cat

doll   bee   deer

Ending Sound of Dd

Directions: Read the sentence and listen to the sound **d** makes at the end of **dad**, **bread**, and **bed**. Name all the pictures out loud. Then, circle the pictures that end with the /d/ sound.

 Da**d** ate brea**d** in be**d**.

sled   lid   ball

cat   lizard   wood

boot   bird   sad

Name _____

Review Beginning Bb, Cc, and Dd Sounds

Directions: Name all the pictures. Then, draw a line from each picture to its beginning sound.

duck

bed

cent

bell

dime

cat

doll

ball

car

circle

/b/

/k/

/s/

/d/

Review Ending Bb, Cc, and Dd Sounds

Directions: Name all the pictures. Then, draw a line from each picture to its ending sound.

picnic

tub

sled

wood

/b/

bird

traffic

crab

/k/

garlic

web

/d/

Beginning Sound of Ff

Directions: Say the name of each picture. Then, circle each picture that begins with the /f/ sound.

fish

fox

fan

leaf

fence

turtle

Ending Sound of Ff

Directions: Say the name of each picture. Then, circle each picture that ends with the /f/ sound.

leaf

roof

hoof

scarf

bread

cat

elf

wolf

surf

Beginning Sound of Gg

Directions: Say the name of each picture. Then, circle each picture that begins with the /g/ sound.

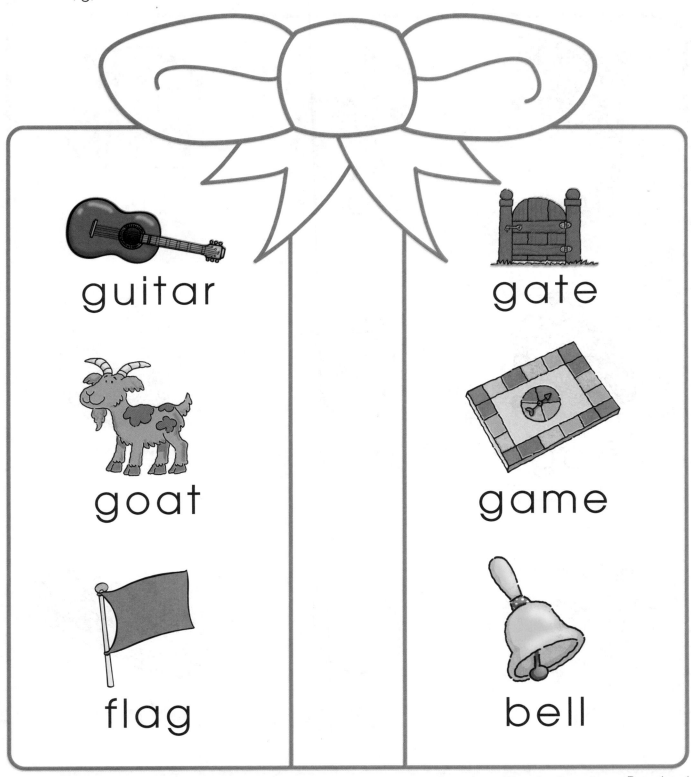

guitar

gate

goat

game

flag

bell

Ending Sound of Gg

Directions: Say the name of each picture. Then, circle each picture that ends with the /g/ sound.

flag   goat   bag

frog   mug   apple

pig   egg   log

Beginning Sound of Hh

Directions: Say the name of each picture. Then, circle each picture that begins with the /h/ sound.

hat

horse

hop

goat

hit

hand

hive

hose

kangaroo

Review Beginning Sounds of Ff, Gg, and Hh

Directions: Say the sound in each box. Then, circle each picture that begins with that sound.

/f/	raccoon	fence	fox
/g/	goat	bag	gate
/h/	roof	hive	horse

Name _____

Review Ending Sounds of Ff and Gg

Directions: Say the sound in each box. Then, circle each picture that ends with that sound.

leaf   frog   scarf   /f/

goat   flag   pig   /g/

Beginning Sound of Jj

Directions: Say the name of each picture. Then, circle each picture that begins with the /j/ sound.

jar   jam   jet

jump rope   jack-in-the-box

grapes   pup   jacket

Ending Sound of Jj

Directions: Say the name of each picture. Notice that the letters **ge** make the /j/ sound at the end of each word. Circle each picture that ends with the /j/ sound.

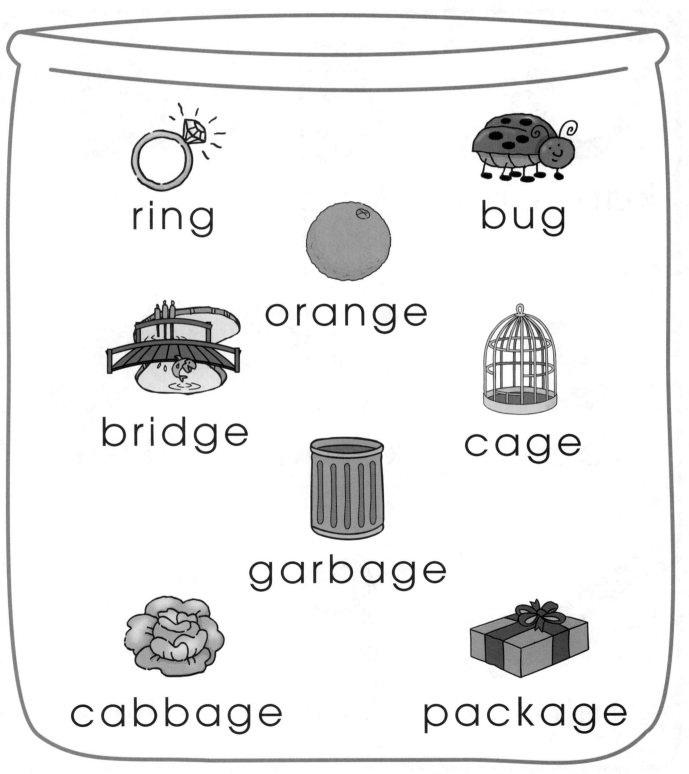

ring

orange

bug

bridge

cage

garbage

cabbage

package

Name _____

Beginning Sound of Kk

Directions: Say the name of each picture. Then, circle each picture that begins with the /k/ sound.

kangaroo king tape

  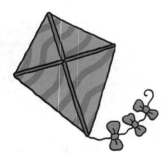

robe kitten kite

ruler key kick

Name _____

Ending Sound of Kk

Directions: Say the name of each picture. Then, circle each picture that ends with the /k/ sound.

truck

duck

hook

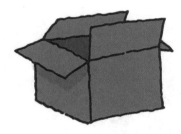
box

clock

lock

book

basket

fork

Spectrum Phonics Readiness Preschool

63

Beginning Sound of Ll

Directions: Say the name of each picture. Then, cross out each picture that does not begin with the /l/ sound.

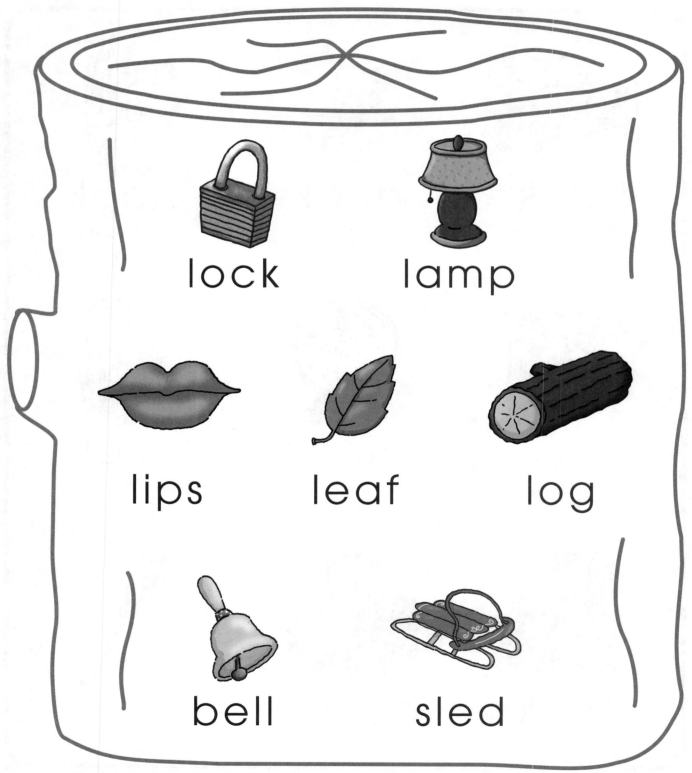

lock   lamp

lips   leaf   log

bell   sled

Name _____

Ending Sound of Ll

Directions: Say the name of each picture. Then, cross out each name that does not end with the /l/ sound.

bell

log

well

bowl

doll

clock

milk

snail

drill

Review Beginning Sounds
of Jj, Kk, and Ll

Directions: Say the name of the picture in the first box of a row. Listen for the beginning sound. Then, name the other pictures in the row. Find and circle the pictures in the row that have the same beginning sound.

jar	grapes	jet	jam
key	kite	kitten	milk
lock	leaf	doll	lamp

Name _____

Review Ending Sounds
of Jj, Kk, and Ll

Directions: Say the name of the picture in the first box of a row. Listen for the ending sound. Then, name the other pictures in the row. Find and circle the pictures in the row that have the same ending sound.

orange	leaf	cage	cabbage
truck	hook	book	box
bowl	snail	drill	log

Beginning Sound of Mm

Directions: Say the name all each picture. Then, cross out each picture that does not begin with the /m/ sound.

milk

lamp

kangaroo

moon

mouse

mug

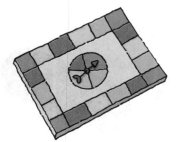
game

map

mirror

Name _____

Ending Sound of Mm

Directions: Say the name of each picture. Then, cross out each picture that does not end with the /m/ sound.

rake

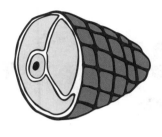
ham

broom

jam

plum

mirror

drum

swim

moose

Beginning Sound of Nn

Directions: Say the name of each picture. Then, cross out each picture that does not begin with the /n/ sound.

pan   nest   yarn

nut   nose   note

sun   spoon   nickel

Ending Sound of Nn

Directions: Say the name of each picture. Then, cross out each picture that does not end with the /n/ sound.

pan

can

man

bike

hen

pen

worm

fan

van

Beginning Sound of Pp

Directions: Say the name of each picture. Then, circle each picture that starts with the /p/ sound.

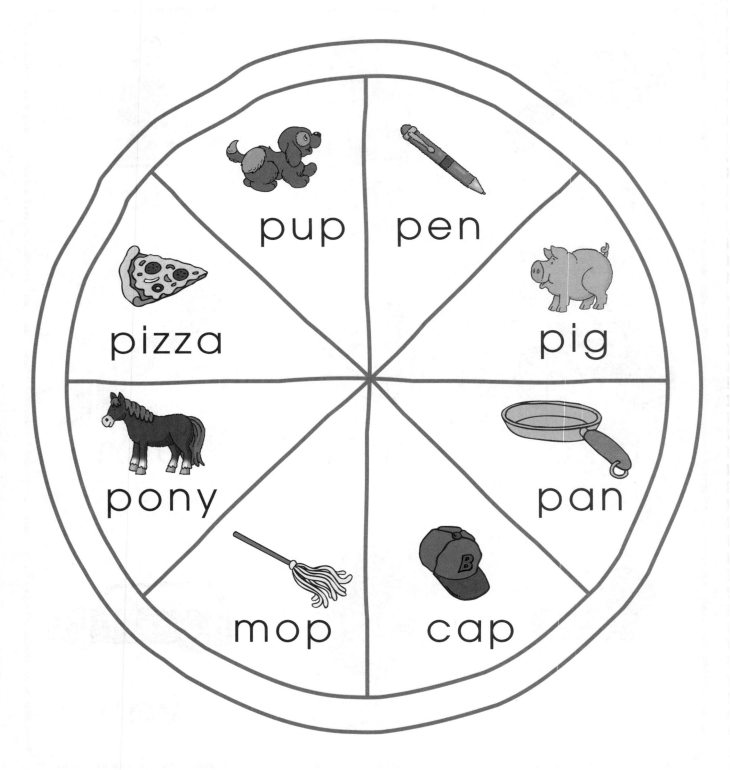

pup   pen

pizza

pig

pony

pan

mop   cap

Name _____

Ending Sound of Pp

Directions: Say the name of each picture. Then, cross out each picture that does not end with the /p/ sound.

lamp

soup

crab

mop

bed

stamp

top

scarf

cup

Review Beginning Sounds of Mm, Nn, and Pp

Directions: Say the name of the picture in the first box of the first column. Listen for the beginning sound. Then, circle each picture in the column that has the same beginning sound.

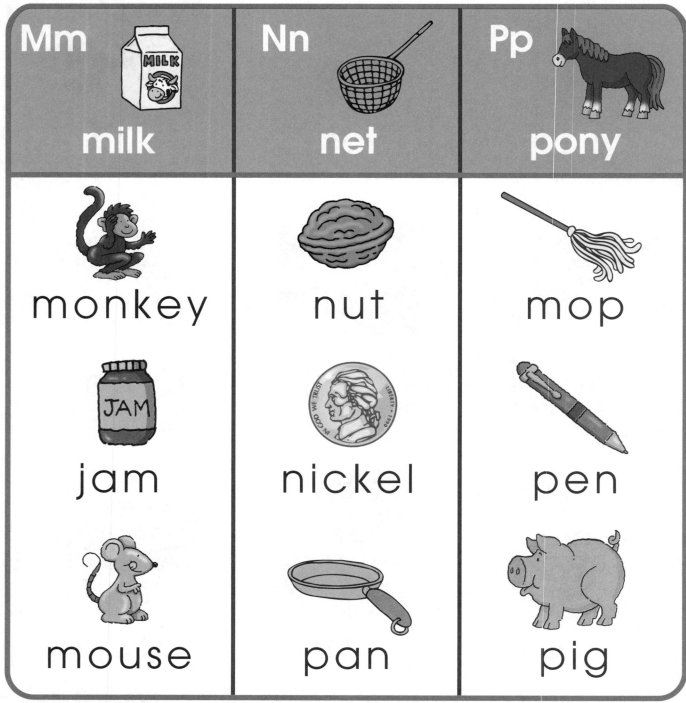

Mm milk	Nn net	Pp pony
monkey	nut	mop
jam	nickel	pen
mouse	pan	pig

Name _____

Review Ending Sounds
of Mm, Nn, and Pp

Directions: Say the name of the picture in the first box of the first column. Listen for the ending sound. Then, circle each picture in the column that has the same ending sound.

Mm	Nn	Pp
plum	hen	mop
drum	nest	stamp
broom	fan	spoon
man	can	cap

Beginning Sound of Qq

Directions: Say the name of each picture. Then, cross out each picture that does not begin with the /q/ sound.

quarter

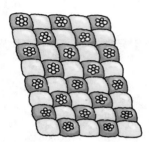
quilt

fish

queen

guitar

quack

quail

goat

Beginning Sound of Rr

Directions: Say the name of each picture. Then, circle each picture that begins with the /r/ sound.

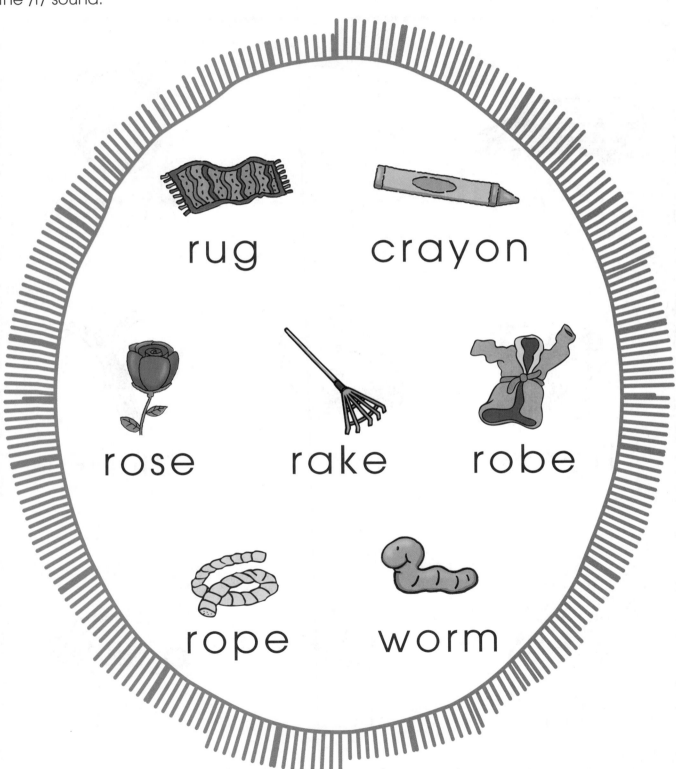

rug   crayon

rose   rake   robe

rope   worm

Ending Sound of Rr

Directions: Say the name of each picture. Then, cross out each picture that does not end with the /r/ sound.

van

jar

mirror

tiger

frog

zipper

star

top

car

Beginning Sound of Ss

Directions: Say the name of each picture. Then, cross out each picture that does not begin with the /s/ sound.

sand   sun   bus

flag   ~il~   moose

s~~   ~~k   saw

Ending Sound of Ss

Directions: Say the name of each picture. Then, cross out each picture that does not end with the /s/ sound.

bus

lock

grapes

skates

dress

sled

cactus

lips

fish

Review Beginning Sounds
of Qq, Rr, and Ss

Directions: Say the name of each picture. Listen to the beginning sound. Then, draw a line to match each picture with its beginning sound.

sand

raccoon   **/ q /**

quarter

quilt

rug    **/ r /**

seal

rose

sun   **/ s /**

queen

Review Ending Sounds
of Rr and Ss

Directions: Say the name of each picture. Listen to the ending sound. Then, draw a line to match each picture with its ending sound.

mirror

grapes

tiger

dress

bus

zipper

/ r /

/ s /

Name _____

Beginning Sound of Tt

Directions: Say the name of each picture. Then, circle each picture that begins with the /t/ sound.

table

turtle

tiger

top

tub

coat

tape

star

boat

Ending Sound of Tt

Directions: Say the name of each picture. Then, cross out each picture that does not end with the /t/ sound.

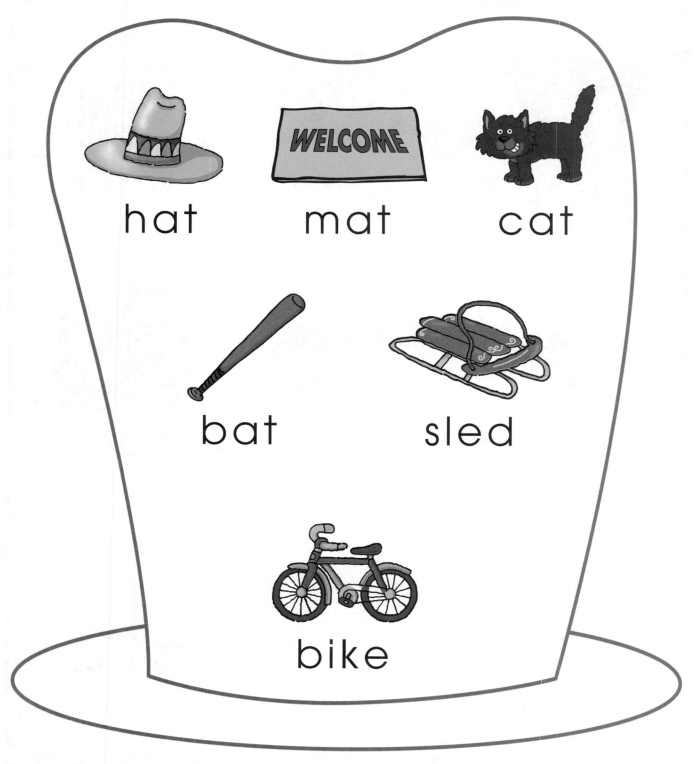

hat   mat   cat

bat   sled

bike

Beginning Sound of Vv

Directions: Say the name of each picture. Then, cross out each picture that does not begin with the /v/ sound.

van

vest

nest

vine

win

vase

fan

violin

vegetables

Beginning Sound of Ww

Directions: Say the name of each picture. Then, circle each picture that begins with the /w/ sound.

vine

wave

watch

wing

van

wire

monkey

win

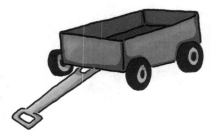
wagon

Name _____

Review Beginning Sounds
of Tt, Vv, and Ww

Directions: Say the sound in each box. Then, circle each picture that begins with that sound.

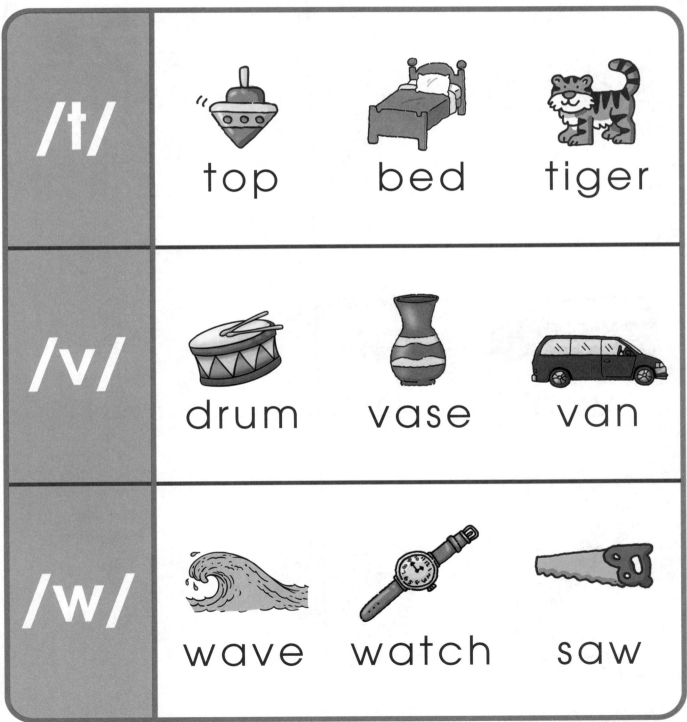

/t/	top	bed	tiger
/v/	drum	vase	van
/w/	wave	watch	saw

Name _____

Review Ending Sound of Tt

Directions: Say the name of each picture. Then, circle each picture that ends with the /t/ sound.

hat

bat

lizard

van

pizza

net

crayon

drum

hit

Beginning Sound of Xx

Directions: Say the name of each picture. Notice that sometimes the /x/ sound is spelled **ex** at the beginning of a word. Cross out each picture that does not begin with the /x/ sound.

exercise

saw

exit

van

web

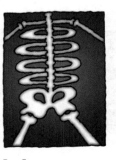

X-ray

Ending Sound of Xx

Directions: Say the name of each picture. Notice that **x** makes a /ks/ sound when it comes at the end of a word. Circle each picture that ends with the /x/ sound.

box

pig

fox

block

ax

ox

clock

log

mix

Name _____

Beginning Sound of Yy

Directions: Say the name of each picture. Then, cross out each picture that does not begin with the /y/ sound.

yo-yo

yellow

yarn

yolk

tub

yummy

worm

vine

yawn

Beginning Sound of Zz

Directions: Say the name of each picture. Then, circle each picture that begins with the /z/ sound.

zero

stamp

zebra

xylophone

zoo

taxicab

sled

zipper

Ending Sound of Zz

Directions: Say the name of each picture. Notice that sometimes the /z/ sound is spelled **ze**. Cross out each picture that does not end with the /z/ sound.

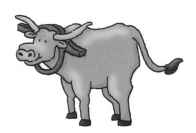
ox

graze

buzz

pop

prize

sock

grapes

fuzz

size

Name _____

Review Beginning Sounds
of Xx, Yy, and Zz

Directions: Say the name of each picture. Draw a line to match each picture with its beginning sound.

zipper

yarn

exit

zoo

X-ray

yo-yo

/x/

/y/

/z/

Review Ending Sounds
of Xx and Zz

Directions: Say the name of each picture. Draw a line from each picture to its ending sound.

box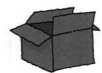

graze    **/ x /**

ox

buzz

fox    **/ z /**

prize

Beginning Sounds

Directions: Say the sound and the name of each picture in a row. Then, circle each picture that begins with that letter sound.

/b/	bell	car	bed
/s/	sun	sock	bus
/n/	skunk	nest	nut
/d/	doll	bee	duck
/t/	tiger	tub	coat

Ending Sounds

Directions: Say the name of each picture and the sound at the end of each row. Then, circle each picture that ends with that letter sound.

bread	leaf	scarf	**/f/**
jar	frog	tiger	**/r/**
bell	top	snail	**/l/**
mirror	drum	broom	**/m/**
truck	book	lizard	**/k/**

Name _____

Long a Sound

Directions: Say the name of each picture. Then, circle each picture that has the long **a** sound.

r**a**ke

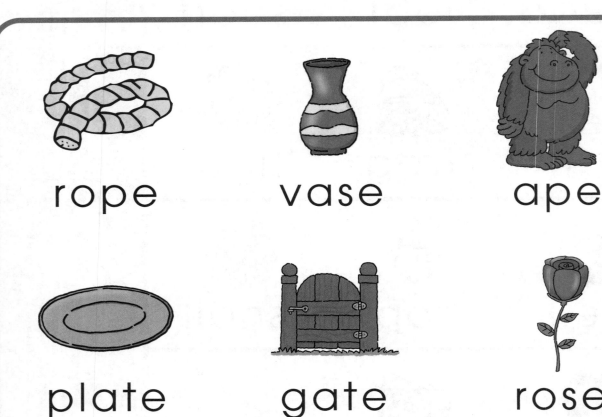

rope   vase   ape

plate   gate   rose

cave   cake   cane

Long e Sound

Directions: Say the name of each picture. Notice that the long **e** sound can be spelled **ea** or **ee**. Circle each picture that has the long **e** sound.

p**ea**s

sh**ee**p

seal

dress

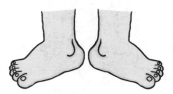

feet

tea

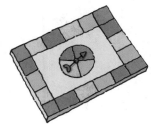

game

leaf

cheek

seat

plate

Long i Sound

Directions: Say the name of each picture. Then, circle each picture that has the long **i** sound.

bike

bear

wave

kite

bite

rose

street

vine

slide

cage

Long o Sound

Directions: Say the name of each picture. Then, circle each picture that has the long **o** sound.

n**o**se

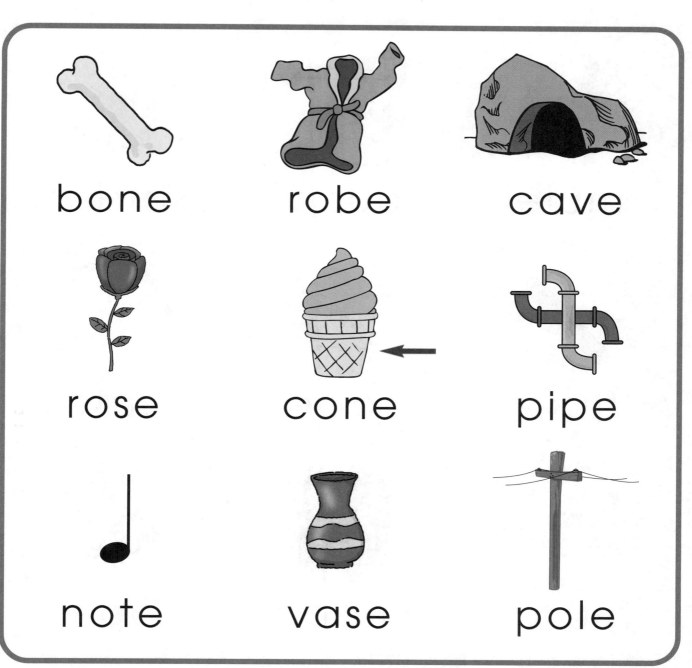

bone   robe   cave

rose   cone   pipe

note   vase   pole

Long u Sound

Directions: Say the name of each picture. Then, circle each picture that has the long **u** sound.

unicorn

mule

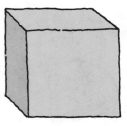

cube

spider

flute

tape

cute

music

menu

bee

Long a, e, and i Sounds

Directions: Say the name of each picture. Draw a line to match each picture with its long vowel sound.

bike

feet

rake

cake

kite

leaf

long a

long e

long i

Long o and u Sounds

Directions: Say the name of each picture. Draw a line to match each picture with its vowel sound.

rose

mule

long o

cone →

cube

flute

long u

hose

Answer Key

Directions: Name the pictures out loud. Then, circle the **a** in each name.

apple   grapes   ant

yarn   hat   pan

ball   alligator   ax

Spectrum Phonics Readiness Preschool

5

Directions: Name the pictures out loud. Then, circle the **b** in each name.

book   rabbit

zebra   bee

comb   bird

Spectrum Phonics Readiness Preschool

6

Directions: Name the pictures out loud. Then, color the **c** in each name.

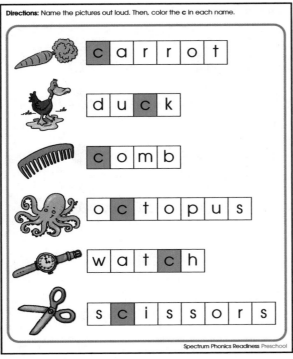

| c | a | r | r | o | t |

| d | u | c | k |

| c | o | m | b |

| o | c | t | o | p | u | s |

| w | a | t | c | h |

| s | c | i | s | s | o | r | s |

Spectrum Phonics Readiness Preschool

7

Directions: Name the pictures out loud. Then, circle the **d** in each name.

deer   bird   sled

bed   duck

lid   dime   bread

Spectrum Phonics Readiness Preschool

8

Answer Key

Five little monkeys jumping on the bed,
One fell off and bumped his head.
Four little monkeys jumping on the bed,
One fell off and bumped his head.
Three little monkeys jumping on the bed,
One fell off and bumped his head.
Two little monkeys jumping on the bed,
One fell off and bumped his head.
One little monkey jumping on the bed,
He fell off and bumped his head.

Spectrum Phonics Readiness Preschool

10

teeth   feet   nose

ear   eye

fingers   elbow   knee

Spectrum Phonics Readiness Preschool

11

football   leaf

fox   giraffe

frog   butterfly

Spectrum Phonics Readiness Preschool

12

grapes   yogurt

eggs   orange

graham crackers

Spectrum Phonics Readiness Preschool

13

Answer Key

Good night, sleep tight.
Wake up bright
In the morning light
To do what's right
With all your might.

Spectrum Phonics Readiness Preschool

14

Spectrum Phonics Readiness Preschool

15

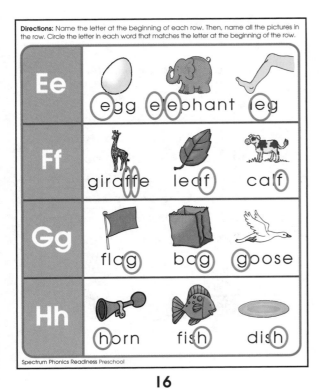

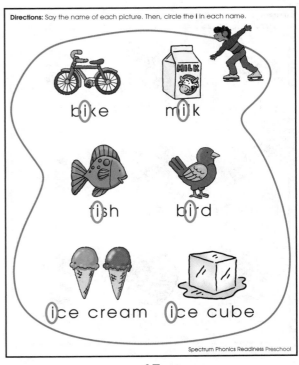

Spectrum Phonics Readiness Preschool

16

Spectrum Phonics Readiness Preschool

17

Answer Key

Directions: Say the name of each picture. Then, underline each **j** you find.

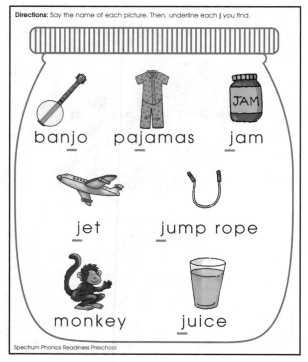

banjo   pajamas   jam

jet   jump rope

monkey   juice

Spectrum Phonics Readiness Preschool

18

Directions: Say the name of each picture. Then, circle the **k** in each name. Underline each animal.

key

duck   fork   kitten

bike

Spectrum Phonics Readiness Preschool

19

Directions: Say the name of each picture. Then, underline the **l** in each name.

lock   butterfly   lips

balloon   pencil   lamb

candle   apple   lamp

Spectrum Phonics Readiness Preschool

20

Directions: Read "Mary Had a Little Lamb." Then, underline the rhyming words in the poem.

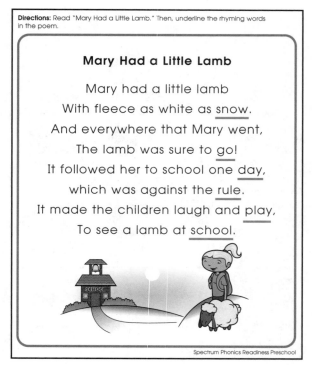

Mary Had a Little Lamb

Mary had a little lamb
With fleece as white as snow.
And everywhere that Mary went,
The lamb was sure to go!
It followed her to school one day,
which was against the rule.
It made the children laugh and play,
To see a lamb at school.

Spectrum Phonics Readiness Preschool

21

Spectrum Phonics Readiness Preschool

Answer Key

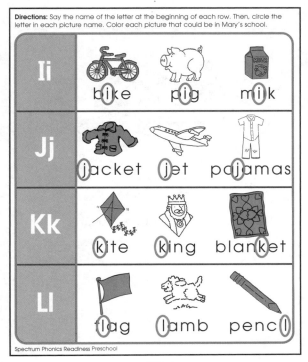

Directions: Say the name of the letter at the beginning of each row. Then, circle the letter in each picture name. Color each picture that could be in Mary's school.

Ii	bike	pig	milk
Jj	jacket	jet	pajamas
Kk	kite	king	blanket
Ll	flag	lamb	pencil

Spectrum Phonics Readiness Preschool

22

Directions: Say the name of each picture. Then, draw a line under the **m** in each name. Draw an **X** on each animal.

milk lamb drum

nut moon moose

mouse dime monkey

Spectrum Phonics Readiness Preschool

23

Directions: Say the name of each picture. Then, draw a line under the **n** in each name.

hen pin pan

bun man fan

nut van can

Spectrum Phonics Readiness Preschool

24

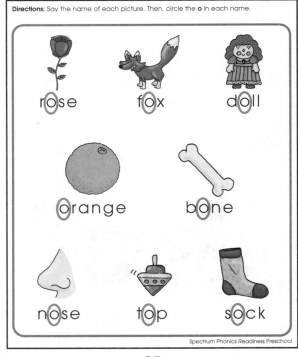

Directions: Say the name of each picture. Then, circle the **o** in each name.

rose fox doll

orange bone

nose top sock

Spectrum Phonics Readiness Preschool

25

Answer Key

Directions: Say the name of each picture. Then, circle the **p** in each name. Underline each piece of fruit.

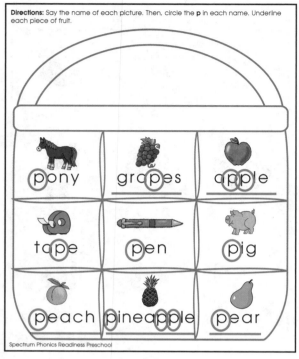

pony   grapes   apple

tape   pen   pig

peach   pineapple   pear

Spectrum Phonics Readiness Preschool

26

Directions: Read "Pat-a-Cake." Underline the words that rhyme.

Pat-a-Cake

Pat-a-cake, pat-a-cake, baker's <u>man</u>,
Bake me a cake as fast as you <u>can</u>.
Pat it and smooth it and mark it with a **B**,
And put it in the oven for baby and <u>me</u>.

Spectrum Phonics Readiness Preschool

27

Directions: Circle each **m**, **n**, **o**, and **p** in the poem.

Pat-a-Cake

Pat-a-cake, pat-a-cake, baker's man
Bake me a cake as fast as you can
Pat it and smooth it and mark it with a **B**,
And put it in the oven for baby and me.

Spectrum Phonics Readiness Preschool

28

Directions: Say the name of each picture. Then, circle the **q** in each name.

quarter   quilt   queen

quack   question   quail

squid   quiet   square

Spectrum Phonics Readiness Preschool

29

Answer Key

Directions: Say the name of each picture. Then, color the **r** in each name. Circle each thing that rolls.

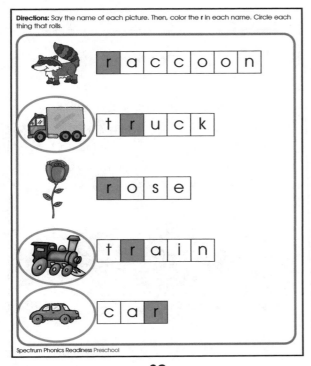

| r | a | c | c | o | o | n |

| t | r | u | c | k |

| r | o | s | e |

| t | r | a | i | n |

| c | a | r |

Spectrum Phonics Readiness Preschool

30

Directions: Say the name of each picture. Then, circle the **s** in each name.

snake spider snail

starfish fish moose

horse skunk seal

Spectrum Phonics Readiness Preschool

31

Directions: Say the name of each picture. Then, draw a line under the **t** in each name.

turtle tiger tent

jet nut

tape coat tub

Spectrum Phonics Readiness Preschool

32

Directions: Say the name of each picture. Then, circle the **u** in each name.

umbrella bus rug

tub drum sun

puppy unhappy brush

Spectrum Phonics Readiness Preschool

33

Answer Key

Directions: Read "Six Little Ducks." Then, underline the words that rhyme.

Six Little Ducks

Six little ducks that I once <u>knew</u>;
Black ones, brown ones, white ones, <u>too</u>.
But the one little duck with the feather on his <u>back</u>,
He led the others with a *<u>quack</u>, <u>quack</u>, <u>quack</u>.*
<u>quack</u>, <u>quack</u>, <u>quack</u>—<u>quack</u>, <u>quack</u>, <u>quack</u>.
He led the others with a *<u>quack</u>, <u>quack</u>, <u>quack</u>.*

Spectrum Phonics Readiness Preschool

34

Directions: Circle each **q, r, s, t,** and **u** in the poem.

Six Little Ducks

Six little ducks that I once knew;
Black ones, brown ones, white ones, too.
But the one little duck with the feather on his back,
He led the others with a quack, quack, quack.
quack, quack, quack—quack, quack, quack.
He led the others with a quack, quack, quack.

Spectrum Phonics Readiness Preschool

35

Directions: Name all the pictures. Then, circle the **v** in each name.

cave   van   vest

dive   vine   wave

vase   hive   violin

Spectrum Phonics Readiness Preschool

36

Directions: Name all the pictures. Then, circle the **w** in each name.

wave   swim   snow

sweater   crown   whistle

watch   swing   wash

Spectrum Phonics Readiness Preschool

37

Answer Key

Directions: Name all the pictures. Then, color the **x** in each name.

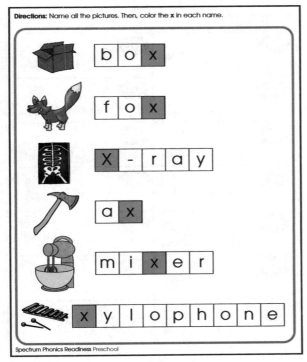

- b o **x**
- f o **x**
- **x** - r a y
- a **x**
- m i **x** e r
- **x** y l o p h o n e

Directions: Name all the pictures. Then, circle the **y** in each name.

pon(y) pupp(y) lad(y)

(y)awn sk(y) cr(y)

(y)o-(y)o (y)arn bab(y)

Directions: Name all the pictures. Then, color the **z** in each name.

- **z** i p p e r
- **z** e b r a
- l i **z** a r d
- m a g a **z** i n e

Directions: Draw a line to match the uppercase and lowercase letters.

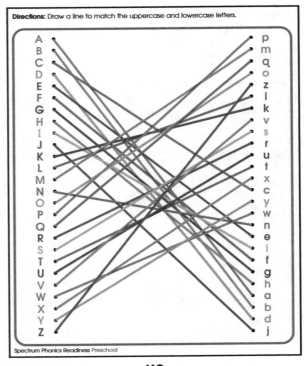

A B C D E F G H I J K L M N O P Q R S T U V W X Y Z

p m q o z l k v s r u t x c y w n e i f g h a b d j

Answer Key

Directions: Name all the letters and pictures. Then, find the letter in each name and draw a line under it.

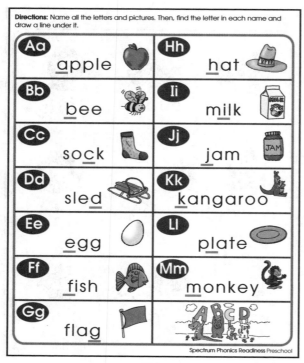

Aa — _apple
Bb — _bee
Cc — so_ck
Dd — sle_d
Ee — _egg
Ff — _fish
Gg — fla_g
Hh — _hat
Ii — m_ilk
Jj — _jam
Kk — _kangaroo
Ll — p_late
Mm — _monkey

43

Directions: Name all the letters and pictures. Then, find the letter in each name and draw a line under it.

Nn — pa_n
Oo — d_oll
Pp — _tape
Qq — _queen
Rr — f_rog
Ss — _saw
Tt — _tiger
Uu — bu_s
Vv — _vase
Ww — _snow
Xx — bo_x
Yy — pupp_y
Zz — _zebra

44

Directions: Listen to the /b/ sound at the beginning of **boy**, **bat**, and **ball**. Circle the names that begin with the /b/ sound.

This **b**oy can **b**at the **b**all.

balloon | cat | banana
bat | car | ball
dog | bed | bell

45

Directions: Read the sentence and listen to the /b/ sound at the end of **scrub** and **tub**. Then, circle the pictures that end with the /b/ sound.

I will scru**b** the tu**b**.

tub | crab | mug
bib | web | tape
taxicab | red | doorknob

46

Answer Key

Spectrum Phonics Readiness Preschool

Directions: When **c** comes at the beginning of a word, sometimes it makes an /s/ sound and sometimes it makes a /k/ sound. Say each word out loud. Underline the pictures that begin with a **c** that makes an /s/ sound. Then, circle the pictures that begin with a **c** that makes the /k/ sound.

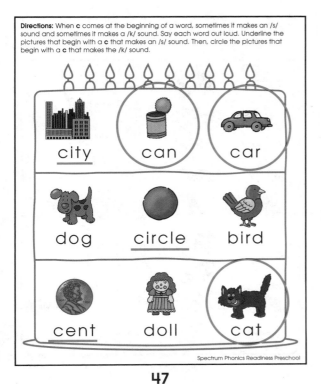

city   can   car

dog   circle   bird

cent   doll   cat

Spectrum Phonics Readiness Preschool

47

Directions: When **c** is at the end of a word, it makes the /k/ sound. Say each word out loud. Circle each picture that ends with a **c** that makes the /k/ sound.

traffic   garlic

picnic   tub

bed   pig

Spectrum Phonics Readiness Preschool

48

Directions: Read the words out loud. Cross out any picture that does not begin with the /d/ sound.

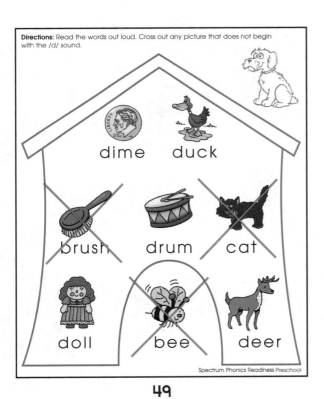

dime   duck

brush   drum   cat

doll   bee   deer

Spectrum Phonics Readiness Preschool

49

Directions: Read the sentence and listen to the sound **d** makes at the end of **dad**, **bread**, and **bed**. Name all the pictures out loud. Then, circle the pictures that end with the /d/ sound.

Da**d** ate brea**d** in be**d**.

sled   lid   ball

cat   lizard   wood

boot   bird   sad

Spectrum Phonics Readiness Preschool

50

Answer Key

Directions: Name all the pictures. Then, draw a line from each picture to its beginning sound.

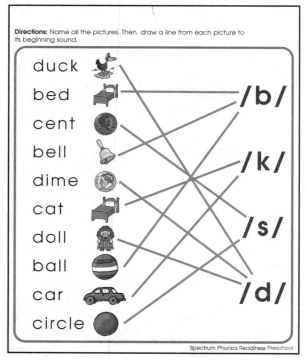

duck
bed
cent
bell
dime
cat
doll
ball
car
circle

/b/
/k/
/s/
/d/

Spectrum Phonics Readiness Preschool

51

Directions: Name all the pictures. Then, draw a line from each picture to its ending sound.

picnic
tub
sled
wood
bird
traffic
crab
garlic
web

/b/
/k/
/d/

Spectrum Phonics Readiness Preschool

52

Directions: Say the name of each picture. Then, circle each picture that begins with the /f/ sound.

fish   fox
fan   leaf
fence   turtle

Spectrum Phonics Readiness Preschool

53

Directions: Say the name of each picture. Then, circle each picture that ends with the /f/ sound.

leaf   roof   hoof
scarf   bread   cat
elf   wolf   surf

Spectrum Phonics Readiness Preschool

54

Answer Key

Directions: Say the name of each picture. Then, circle each picture that begins with the /g/ sound.

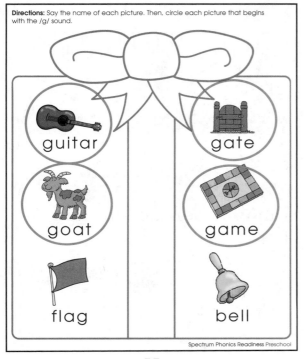

55

Directions: Say the name of each picture. Then, circle each picture that ends with the /g/ sound.

flag	goat	bag
frog	mug	apple
pig	egg	log

Spectrum Phonics Readiness Preschool

56

Directions: Say the name of each picture. Then, circle each picture that begins with the /h/ sound.

57

Directions: Say the sound in each box. Then, circle each picture that begins with that sound.

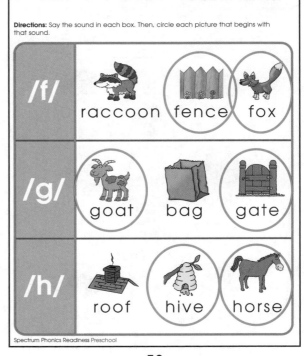

58

Answer Key

Directions: Say the sound in each box. Then, circle each picture that ends with that sound.

leaf   frog   scarf   **/f/**

goat   flag   pig   **/g/**

Spectrum Phonics Readiness Preschool

59

Directions: Say the name of each picture. Then, circle each picture that begins with the /j/ sound.

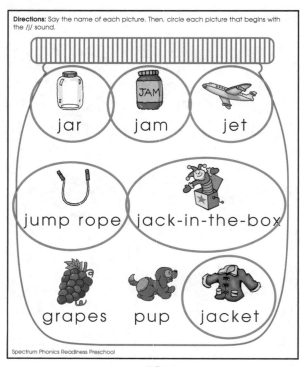

jar   jam   jet

jump rope   jack-in-the-box

grapes   pup   jacket

Spectrum Phonics Readiness Preschool

60

Directions: Say the name of each picture. Notice that the letters **ge** make the /j/ sound at the end of each word. Circle each picture that ends with the /j/ sound.

ring   bug   orange   bridge   cage   garbage   cabbage   package

Spectrum Phonics Readiness Preschool

61

Directions: Say the name of each picture. Then, circle each picture that begins with the /k/ sound.

kangaroo   king   tape

robe   kitten   kite

ruler   key   kick

Spectrum Phonics Readiness Preschool

62

Spectrum Phonics Readiness Preschool

Answer Key

Directions: Say the name of each picture. Then, circle each picture that ends with the /k/ sound.

truck · duck · hook · box · clock · lock · book · basket · fork

Spectrum Phonics Readiness Preschool

63

Directions: Say the name of each picture. Then, cross out each picture that does not begin with the /l/ sound.

lock · lamp · lips · leaf · log · bell · sled

Spectrum Phonics Readiness Preschool

64

Directions: Say the name of each picture. Then, cross out each name that does not end with the /l/ sound.

bell · log · well · bowl · doll · clock · milk · snail · drill

Spectrum Phonics Readiness Preschool

65

Directions: Say the name of the picture in the first box of a row. Listen for the beginning sound. Then, name the other pictures in the row. Find and circle the pictures in the row that have the same beginning sound.

jar · grapes · jet · jam
key · kite · kitten · milk
lock · leaf · doll · lamp

Spectrum Phonics Readiness Preschool

66

Answer Key

Directions: Say the name of the picture in the first box of a row. Listen for the ending sound. Then, name the other pictures in the row. Find and circle the pictures in the row that have the same ending sound.

orange	leaf	cage	cabbage
truck	hook	book	box
bowl	snail	drill	log

Spectrum Phonics Readiness Preschool

67

Directions: Say the name all each picture. Then, cross out each picture that does not begin with the /m/ sound.

milk — lamp — kangaroo

moon — mouse — mug

game — map — mirror

Spectrum Phonics Readiness Preschool

68

Directions: Say the name of each picture. Then, cross out each picture that does not end with the /m/ sound.

rake — ham — broom

jam — plum — mirror

drum — swim — moose

Spectrum Phonics Readiness Preschool

69

Directions: Say the name of each picture. Then, cross out each picture that does not begin with the /n/ sound.

pan — nest — yarn

nut — nose — note

sun — spoon — nickel

Spectrum Phonics Readiness Preschool

70

Answer Key

Directions: Say the name of each picture. Then, cross out each picture that does not end with the /n/ sound.

pan   can   man

~~bike~~   hen   pen

~~worm~~   fan   van

Spectrum Phonics Readiness Preschool

71

Directions: Say the name of each picture. Then, circle each picture that starts with the /p/ sound.

pup   pen

pizza   pig

pony   pan

mop   cap

Spectrum Phonics Readiness Preschool

72

Directions: Say the name of each picture. Then, cross out each picture that does not end with the /p/ sound.

lamp   soup   ~~crab~~

mop   ~~bed~~   stamp

top   ~~scarf~~   cup

Spectrum Phonics Readiness Preschool

73

Directions: Say the name of the picture in the first box of the first column. Listen for the beginning sound. Then, circle each picture in the column that has the same beginning sound.

Mm	Nn	Pp
milk	net	pony
monkey	nut	mop
jam	nickel	pen
mouse	pan	pig

Spectrum Phonics Readiness Preschool

74

Answer Key

Directions: Say the name of the picture in the first box of the first column. Listen for the ending sound. Then, circle each picture in the column that has the same ending sound.

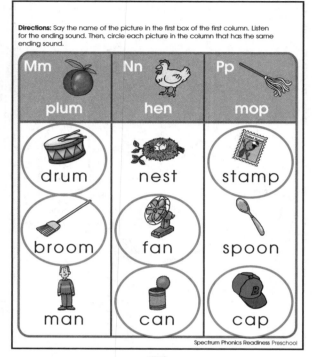

Mm	Nn	Pp
plum	hen	mop
drum	nest	stamp
broom	fan	spoon
man	can	cap

Spectrum Phonics Readiness Preschool

75

Directions: Say the name of each picture. Then, cross out each picture that does not begin with the /q/ sound.

quarter   quilt   fish

queen   guitar

quack   quail   goat

Spectrum Phonics Readiness Preschool

76

Directions: Say the name of each picture. Then, circle each picture that begins with the /r/ sound.

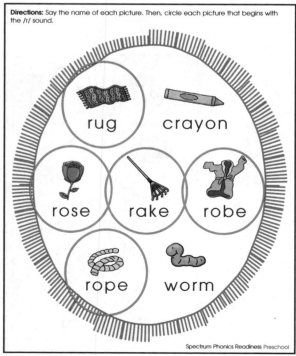

rug   crayon

rose   rake   robe

rope   worm

Spectrum Phonics Readiness Preschool

77

Directions: Say the name of each picture. Then, cross out each picture that does not end with the /r/ sound.

van   jar   mirror

tiger   frog   zipper

star   top   car

Spectrum Phonics Readiness Preschool

78

Answer Key

Directions: Say the name of each picture. Then, cross out each picture that does not begin with the /s/ sound.

sand   sun   bus

flag   snail   moose

seal   sock   saw

Spectrum Phonics Readiness Preschool

79

Directions: Say the name of each picture. Then, cross out each picture that does not end with the /s/ sound.

bus   lock   grapes

skates   dress   sled

cactus   lips   fish

Spectrum Phonics Readiness Preschool

80

Directions: Say the name of each picture. Listen to the beginning sound. Then, draw a line to match each picture with its beginning sound.

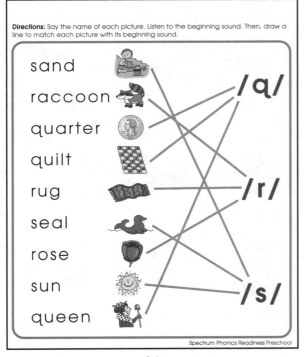

sand
raccoon
quarter
quilt
rug
seal
rose
sun
queen

/q/

/r/

/s/

Spectrum Phonics Readiness Preschool

81

Directions: Say the name of each picture. Listen to the ending sound. Then, draw a line to match each picture with its ending sound.

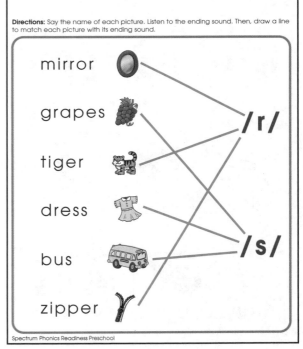

mirror
grapes
tiger
dress
bus
zipper

/r/

/s/

Spectrum Phonics Readiness Preschool

82

Answer Key

Directions: Say the name of each picture. Then, circle each picture that begins with the /t/ sound.

table   turtle   tiger

top   tub   coat

tape   star   boat

Spectrum Phonics Readiness Preschool

83

Directions: Say the name of each picture. Then, cross out each picture that does not end with the /t/ sound.

hat   mat   cat

bat   sled

bike

Spectrum Phonics Readiness Preschool

84

Directions: Say the name of each picture. Then, cross out each picture that does not begin with the /v/ sound.

van   vest   nest

vine   win   vase

fan   violin   vegetables

Spectrum Phonics Readiness Preschool

85

Directions: Say the name of each picture. Then, circle each picture that begins with the /w/ sound.

vine   wave   watch

wing   van   wire

monkey   win   wagon

Spectrum Phonics Readiness Preschool

86

Answer Key

Directions: Say the sound in each box. Then, circle each picture that begins with that sound.

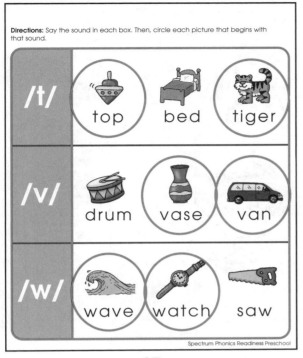

/t/	top	bed	tiger
/v/	drum	vase	van
/w/	wave	watch	saw

Spectrum Phonics Readiness Preschool

87

Directions: Say the name of each picture. Then, circle each picture that ends with the /t/ sound.

hat   bat   lizard

van   pizza   net

crayon   drum   hit

Spectrum Phonics Readiness Preschool

88

Directions: Say the name of each picture. Notice that sometimes the /x/ sound is spelled **ex** at the beginning of a word. Cross out each picture that does not begin with the /x/ sound.

exercise   saw

exit   van

web   X-ray

Spectrum Phonics Readiness Preschool

89

Directions: Say the name of each picture. Notice that **x** makes a /ks/ sound when it comes at the end of a word. Circle each picture that ends with the /x/ sound.

box   pig   fox

block   ax   ox

clock   log   mix

Spectrum Phonics Readiness Preschool

90

Spectrum Phonics Readiness Preschool

125

Answer Key

Directions: Say the name of each picture. Then, cross out each picture that does not begin with the /y/ sound.

yo-yo   yellow   yarn
yolk   tub   yummy
worm   vine   yawn

Spectrum Phonics Readiness Preschool

91

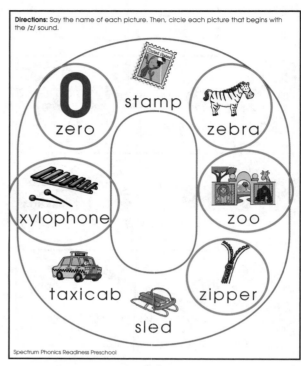

Directions: Say the name of each picture. Then, circle each picture that begins with the /z/ sound.

zero   stamp   zebra
xylophone   zoo
taxicab   zipper
sled

Spectrum Phonics Readiness Preschool

92

Directions: Say the name of each picture. Notice that sometimes the /z/ sound is spelled **ze**. Cross out each picture that does not end with the /z/ sound.

ox   graze   buzz
pop   prize   sock
grapes   fuzz   size

Spectrum Phonics Readiness Preschool

93

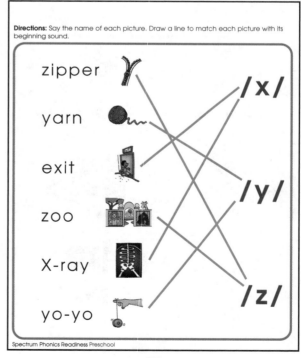

Directions: Say the name of each picture. Draw a line to match each picture with its beginning sound.

zipper
yarn   /x/
exit
zoo   /y/
X-ray
yo-yo   /z/

Spectrum Phonics Readiness Preschool

94

Answer Key

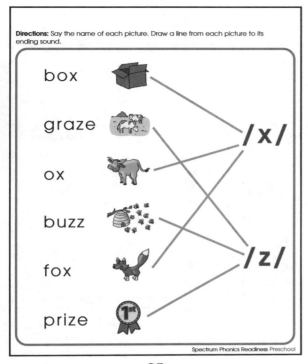
Directions: Say the sound and the name of each picture in a row. Then, circle each picture that begins with that letter sound.

/b/	bell	car	bed
/s/	sun	sock	bus
/n/	skunk	nest	nut
/d/	doll	bee	duck
/t/	tiger	tub	coat

Spectrum Phonics Readiness Preschool

96

Directions: Say the name of each picture and the sound at the end of each row. Then, circle each picture that ends with that letter sound.

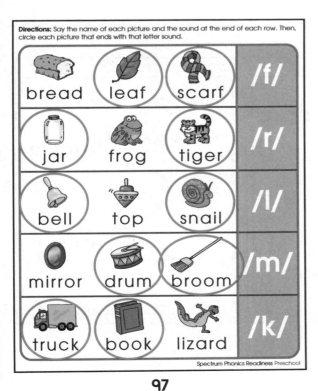

bread	leaf	scarf	/f/
jar	frog	tiger	/r/
bell	top	snail	/l/
mirror	drum	broom	/m/
truck	book	lizard	/k/

Spectrum Phonics Readiness Preschool

97

Directions: Say the name of each picture. Then, circle each picture that has the long **a** sound.

rake

rope   vase   ape

plate   gate   rose

cave   cake   cane

Spectrum Phonics Readiness Preschool

98

Answer Key

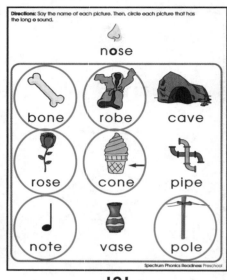

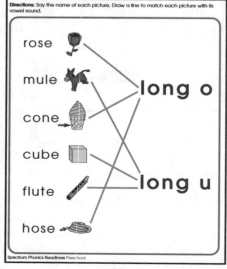